ISBN: 9798829188436
Imprint: Independently published

Contents

Introduction

From childhood through an over eighty-year lifetime these poems range from child-like to mature, stark to beautiful, grief to joy, and light to profound. The 42 new poems begin on page 48 and end on Page 59. There are a total of 275 haiku-like milestones each in as few as eleven and rarely as many as seventeen syllables. Each poem stands on its own. They are not intended to be read as connected to one another except that they are presented in approximate chronological order.

I call these milestones because I stray from the traditional Japanese haiku rules in the following ways:

1. Form is shortened to 11 syllables on 3 lines of 3-5-3 syllables each in order to approximate the traditional Japanese haiku 17 sounds on one line of 5-7-5 sounds with cutting letters, Kireji.
2. Season words are optional not mandatory.
3. Capital letters and punctuation marks are eliminated to focus on sound and sense.
4. Form follows function so alterations in form, capitalization and punctuation at times are made to emphasize sense over form.
5. Apostrophes of possessive and contraction are used when their absence might alter sense.

I do try to follow in Basho's spirit writing these milestones. Practically all translators, linguists, scholars, and leading haiku poets say and show that about 10 to 14 syllables in English is approximately equal to the 17 sounds in Japanese haiku. I chose a 3-5-3 syllable form of 11 syllables to maintain a balance with haiku in Japanese. Here is an example that illustrates my intention: Basho's famous "Frog Pond" haiku in Japanese 5-7-5 syllable form.

> Furu ike ya
> kawazu tobikomu
> mizu no oto

A famous literal American English translation in 3-4-5 syllable lines by R.H. Blyth destroys the 5-7-5 balance of the original:

> The old pond;
> A frog jumps in —
> The sound of the water.

Here's my rather cheeky translation, or maybe more correctly interpretation if you like, in 3-5-3 syllables that preserves the balance and more:

> duckweed pond
> fearless frog jumps in
> ker-PLUNK-plunk

I think this is closer to Basho's intention for these reasons:

1. It emphasizes Basho's allusion to Wang Wei's classical Chinese poem *Duckweed Pond* which we westerner's might otherwise miss.
2. It describes the frog in terms we Westerners understand as the hero and his spiritual journey with the word "fearless" that recalls Don Quixote and Parsifal.
3. It uses the "right" words, which Basho recommends, using onomatopoeia in American English slang "ker-PLUNK-plunk" rather than Blyth's more literal "best" words translation "the sound of water."
4. It capitalizes the first "PLUNK" to visually simulate the louder sound of the first plunk.
5. And it maintains an American English balance of 3-5-3 syllables to Japanese 5-7-5 sounds,

"Genuine poetry can communicate before it is understood" T.S.Eliot

Remember the four levels of understanding:

1. Literal: In a literal manner or sense; exactly what is said, written, or read.

2. Similarity: Similar to, Symbolic of, metaphorical, figurative, representative, or emblematic of our condition.

3. Tradition or Morality: Concerned with our societal or spiritual background.

4. Universality: Oneness pertains to our universal condition.

I hope you have fun reading these little poems slowly, aloud or in meditative silence. Please take some time before reading the next poem and allow it to sink in.

Milestones

when i first
saw over gramma's
windowsill

~

picket fence
pure calvinist white
homestead bound

~

pine needles
iron lawnmower
finger snipped

~

their tall ship
moored to parlor wall
with cobwebs

~

aimlessly
wandering until
dinner call

fallen leaves
stirring in stillness
child giggles

~

back and forth
murmurs from porch swing
fall asleep

~

at midnight
in a firefly flash
gramma's smile

~

reed organ
bach preludes and fugues
then sermons

~

reed organ
pedals and keyboard
far apart

first feeding
i pushed calf to pail
he stiffened

~

second try
hand in milk to mouth
back to pail

~

in our barn
cousin bares her chest
budding breasts

~

slaughtering
necessary but
retching

~

gramma plucks
turkey of feathers
thanksgiving

disappear
its spring barn clean out
cow manure

~

always cold
buttermilk in the
spring house

~

knocked down by
beaver escaping to
the dammed creek

~

sick barn cat
hard to catch and hell
when you do

~

too little
to straddle work horse
i grab mane

learning names
of fish we catch in
beaver creek

~

pheasant shot
one wing still flapping
clobbered dead

~

freshly shot
my uncle skins rabbit
in one stroke

~

picking shot
from buttermilk fried
rabbit

~

haying dust
settles with sunset
wood thrush song

shinnier
clings in ecstasy
flagpole clangs

~

aberdeen
wandering its hills
going forth

~

when i heard
mozart's jupiter
worlds opened

~

father's horn
childhood toy until
mastered

~

piano
improvisations
not practice

a quarter
buys candy popcorn
and western

~

when needed
school stringed bass dusted
tuned and played

~

afternoons
sprawled near radio
operas

~

carl orf and
igor stravinsky
favorites

~

in my hands
well-tempered clavier
ill tempered

thrilled to play
horn in symphony
at fifteen

~

like seigfreid
father left the horn
as nothung

~

my master
shouted play the music
not the notes

~

wind quintet
bach's little fugue lives
just this once

~

song prize goes
to meistersinger
herr wagner

brahms played his
horn trio dreaming
his mother

~

song of songs
orf's in trutina
wedding bliss

~

my nerves ping
hush! ravel's pavane
my horn sings

~

j s bach
is the joy of my
desiring

~

horn quartets
greats and amateurs
swapping parts

rosin dust
veils blushing glances
violin

~

cotton candy
first kiss barely missed
merry-go-round

~

black and brown
piano and gown
warm flesh tones

~

catch opened
fingers still quaking
bra lifted

~

coffee eyes
steep full-bodied cup
swilling cream

enthralled by
a snow queen until
spring breakup

~

denali
shadows her colder
chugach cave

~

on belay
caught too late falling
torn tendon

~

tanana
river under ice
and soldiers

~

eighty miles
over mountains to
warm barracks

skiing in
parade formation in
anchorage

~

on alert
cuban shots completed
bombers roar

~

emptier
than mountain air her
frozen stare

~

climb higher
higher still higher
she's not there

~

a few tears
all too soon it ends
mahler's ninth

words are wedding lace
artful illusion of beauty
veiling beauty's face

~

sunlight streams
through stained glass windows
from her gown

~

veil lifted
shadows of lace still
veil her face

~

fearing heights
goat island's safe but
niagara falls

~

dad, how can
dance so beautiful
hurt so much

une pavane
pour une infante
defunte

~

on tip toe
over me napping
kissing me

~

much depends
on his rain rusted
red wagon

~

his forehead
nuzzles into me
holds on tight

~

hearth cricket
suddenly silent
no child cries

his last breath
as i bend over
to kiss him

~

fresh turned earth
tiny white coffin
red roses

~

angry sky
crackles pops booms snaps
cries and cries

~

the snow queen
unfathomable
haunts me still

~

my son's grave
pure white butterflies
everywhere

on tip toe
over me mourning
he leads

~

furrowed brow
lies fallow until
awakened

~

words words words
conceal dangerous
two-edged swords

~

two diverged
a kiss not taken
telling sigh

~

divorced from
family and friends
gone dc

now divorced
i decorate around
two-crane rug

~

winter shows
but from memory
blossom grows

~

many years
bonsai forest sheds
many tears

~

rise and walk
ugly memories
transfigured

~

seek the truth
find it nowhere but
in yourself

forgetting
all earthly things
just sitting

~

aussie girl
making love before
going out

~

walking to
kennedy center
humming back

~

through snowstorm
christmas with friend and
my daughter

~

even so
she chooses picasso's
self portrait

first longing
breast to chest dances
night long kiss

~

odile or
odette pheromone
confusion

~

how many suns rise
within a dew drenched cobweb
before it dries

~

drunk on her
apricot brandy
flowing free

~

may blossoms
seductively strewn
on perfume

sapphire ring
celebration now
forgotten

~

warming pleas
born on honey breath
of spring tease

~

touching tastes
each other's essence
tenderly

~

the only remains
on his emptied attic floor
dried onion skins

~

fall twilight
yearning for summer's
wood thrush song

on my knees
pale corydalis
pale fireworks

~

song sparrow
bounces each note on
my laughter

~

sunrises
in each dew drop on
spider web

~

christmas wreath
tangled spider's web
raiding wren

~

the whole bay
yet eiders play in
our tide pool

these brambles
bear fruit unlike a
strawberry

~

trillium
crowned with a dew drenched
spider web

~

worn gray fence
wisteria hangs
in shadow

~

trapped fly
spider pounces but
fly escapes

~

less bitter
after the first frost
persimmon

just off the wing tip
beyond that cumulus cloud
some child's red balloon

~

train windows
avoiding glances
in each pane

~

flowing hair
spills apricot brandy
in midair

~

cat purring
curled with her mistress
phone caller

~

world trade center gone
empire state building rises
as i walk to work

fearing heights
fifty stories up
back to glass

~

manhattan
molten amalgam
love and hate

~

meditate
with high-rise windows
burning bright

~

five pilings
for seven seagulls
leapfrogging

~

central park
lincoln center to
scenery change

two chagall's
soften boxiness
at center

~

out in hall
new york phil forgets
mahler's bust

~

lunch in park
opera after
starry night

~

at first light
zendo rock garden
sleeping ox

~

big apple
chess hustlers move in
on each square

scavenging
for last ticket to
rite of spring

~

gone for months
cab horns subway's stench
ah, i'm home

~

fine dining
near kitchen door at
le cirque

~

seven years
no old cells remain
seven times

~

my total
less my transgressions
is just this

ownership
must transcend into
stewardship

~

the smokies
dolloped daily with
fresh whipped clouds

~

at high noon
vulture disappears
in the moon

~

dandelion
parachutes over
smoky mountains

~

shards of day
shattering below
river haze

first fretful
spaniel pacing pen
now released

~

barn stormers
dart dive roll twist spin
barn swallows

~

black vulture
hops on dead pine branch
showering

~

ha! fierce wren
no hose nor sitter
flee or flinch

~

plastic owl
forced to bow under
mocking bird

tail bobbing
pinnacle conquered
mocking bird

~

dammed river
skimmed by skittering
motor boats

~

pesky fly
lands on hand holding
fly swatter

~

breathing in
and out counterpoint
owl hooting

~

galaxies
hundreds of billions
breathing out

returning
waterwheel ladles
sparkling toast

~

poetry
the infinite in
finite words

~

still i see
a cow chewing cud
seeing me

~

gold finches
butterfly-stroke to
raid feeder

~

mountain climbs
on top of itself
into sky

bowing low
to snow laden spruce
bowing too

~

following
fresh wolverine tracks
fearlessly

~

green needles
shelter tangled limbs
arms and legs

~

ring returned
every passerby
has her face

~

at high noon
a half moon rising
no pointing

count to ten
imperturbably
count to ten

~

don't mistake
the pointing finger
for the moon

~

watchmaker
makes every part by hand
to measure time

~

gardener
lets every seed grow
creating time

~

lotus climbs
from slime to sublime
in its time

i will sit
with palms open and
grasp nothing

~

shift eye patch
to see deck or hold
stow aloft

~

wave crashing
no droplet fears drowning
in the sea

~

no answers
just deeper sounding
while sitting

~

dying pine
bears black vultures
just waiting

thermal lifts
vultures just over
me napping

~

silently
snow buries his woods
cardinal sings

~

dragonfly
casts constellations
on ripples

~

duckweed pond
fearless frog jumps in
ker-PLUNK-plunk

~

quiet thoughts
obliterated
blue jay squawks

thistle bent
rocking and bowing
to the sun

~

thanking me
chick-a-dee-dee-dee
scolding me

~

may you be
held in the hollow
of his hand

~

held in the
hollow of his hand
bare her breast

~

opening
blissful gap between
yang and yin

swan descends
deformed goose instead
eye probing

~

zen tells me
that i create a
gateless gate

~

confess then
forgive and forget
and go on

~

when dirty
wash then introduce
a new you

~

there is no
dust on the mirror
no mirror

wonderful
the quiet hours spent
with my self

~

rising from
earth to heavenly
heights sitting

~

sun outlines
drifting cumuli
now a wink

~

gentle waves
weave threads of sunlight
dazzling pool

~

glass half full
alternative fact
half empty

of my time
a smattering of
ignorance

~

pan behind
three graces fountain
ever ogling

~

silhouettes
of mountains through clouds
fog and haze

~

on my knees
peeking under leaves
may apples

~

eleven
syllables can say
everything

love and hate
virtuously solved
compassion

~

mimosa
monarchs mount each bud
quivering

~

mocking bird
teaching his bird calls
to an egg

~

juniper
veiled in ripples
breeze revealed

~

red maple
domes gramma's lilies
all bowing

humming bird tell me
do you delight the lilac
as she delights thee

~

robin nests
on the roof of my
chickadees

~

cumuli
silently traverse
evening sky

~

seam of night
a gander calls me
daydreaming

~

last to sight
wind streaking my hair
with moonlight

when the autumn wind
tucks the last leaf beneath me
bare branches bear stars

~

gardening
every movement creates
new vistas

~

a bee still
on my astilbe
ah, be still

~

loneliness
God, let there be light
she arose

~

sandbox at
gramma's lilac blooms
over her

sandbox dream
sealed with a kiss on
new york street

~

lilac and
brown hair lightly blown
on each kiss

~

wandering
my firefly hunter
leads me home

~

once i wished
upon his bright star
he leads still

~

sky blue eyes
my morning star and
evening star

unnoticed
i watch her blossom
in rose bush

~

soft brushstrokes
sycamore branches
paint our sky

~

song of night
dawns on wayfarer
surge of light

~

my love is
hardened woman and
little girl

~

loves embrace
as flood gates open
shakti's face

love is love
when alteration
tempers it

~

good morning
who calls softly who
mourning dove

~

walk with me softly
do not disturb the dreamer
who dreams you and me

~

her forehead
nuzzles into me
holds on tight

~

hearth cricket
suddenly again
warming heart

cicero
no more tangled books
just gardens

~

stone skitters
across the river
shattering suns

~

inverness
wandering its woods
coming home

~

glasgow road
now paved and lined with
power poles

~

pine tree gone
homestead remodeled
spring runs cold

white chapel
prays over an old
cemetery

~

grave marker
eroded name not
remembered

~

highlandtown
without grave markers
remembered

~

alarm set
to pester gramma
wakes me now

~

my roots in
highlandtown homestead
grow deeper

deadly times
dying without rites
God must cry

~

classmates die
ever more often
fewer mourn

~

hiding from
covid-19 seems
hopeless now

~

sharing sighs
every caress may be
the last one

~

i watch my
garden bloom and die
every day

november
lone golden daisy
still blooming

~

november
scrawny aster feeds
honey bee

~

november
sun on my bare feet
eases pain

~

november
worn arched bridge over
dry creek bed

~

november
pin oak and offspring
holding hands

november
pink camellias through
autumn haze

~

november
golden fans flutter
gingko strips

~

november
a liriope
carousel

~

universe
in a grain of sand
God in man

~

remember
as you and i reach
december

don't you see
that we are seeing
through their eyes

~

meadow nest
musing with crickets
silently

~

corn silk crowns
her buttermilk mound
cherished cave

~

old mountains
are my resting place
wood thrush calls

~

poems slip
between my sleeping
and waking

fall garden
johnny jump ups at
attention

~

crocuses
and tulips buried
for rebirth

~

chickadees
flash in and out of
my wren house

~

butting heads
two vulnerable
loving still

~

stripped of leaves
massive oak displays
old mountains

stripped of leaves
massive oak displays
stars instead

~

autumn rain
washes away my
drying tears

~

birthday gifts
opening deeper
connections

~

wakening
classmates hips ripen
in swimsuit

~

cider press
first pressing guzzled
the best stashed

red and white
billiard balls clack beneath
cigar smoke

~

plain paper
she draws three shadows
sycamore

~

plain paper
one curving black line
two embrace

~

ideas
that survive the night
i write down

~

old lady
in my warm embrace
little girl

first the nits
then things that matter
take your time

~

this gloaming
robins chuck roosting
bats skitter

~

doves huddle
between winter and
spring hoarfrost

~

last years doves
feed at my feet in
periwinkle

~

siren moans
into dead silence
great gate raped

crow murder
shadows exodus
from ukraine

~

rose frozen
in fine porcelean
forever

~

more than sleep
lovely dark and deep
mine to keep

~

his woods burn
but are not consumed
within me

~

ox herding
the struggle begins
over again

as we pass
we hug and kiss 'til
pass again

~

why should i
have such a happy
unending

~

life and death
uninterrupted
life goes on

~

there are many shells
and many more grains of sand
these i leave with you

~

soar vultures
encircle the sun
whirl dervish

on sail on
mirages afore
now astern

Author Keith and his wife Christine McCaughin

About the Author

Keith was born in Lisbon, Ohio in 1939. He was reared in and around this tiny but wonderful town to grow up. He began an early career as a French horn player in several symphony orchestras while he was a junior in high school and continued through conservatory training into mid-life.

He met the love of his life, Christine, and they were and married in 1994.

He earned a BS in Information Systems, and MS in Systems Engineering from Johns Hopkins University. He authored, co-authored and published half-a-dozen papers on enterprise architecture published in various technical journals. In retirement, he published papers on integral politics and chess, a business book *My Consulting Secrets: A Guide to Stakeholder Stewardship Organization and Beyond* and the predecessor to this book of poetry *Little Poems: A lifetime of Haiku-Like Milestones.*

Ruth Cole Review

Author of quite an impressive variety of publications from *Shakespearean Role Models*, a chapter in a book on Shakespeare she was asked to write, to her extensive writing and publishing on Shakespeare, curriculum, gifted education, book reviews, inspirational pieces, and history.

Ruth says about Little Poems: "I'm impressed with your work. The topics are wonderfully wide-ranging; that truly keeps a reader's interest. I hope that there will be more poetry to come. I certainly look forward to reading your future poems. Keep writing."

What Did You Think of More Little Poems?

First of all, thank you for purchasing this book *Little Poems*. I know you could have picked any number of books to read, but you picked this book and for that I am extremely grateful.

I hope that it added at value and quality to your everyday life. If so, it would be really nice if you could share this book with your friends and family by posting to **Facebook** and **Twitter**.

If you enjoyed this book and found some benefit in reading this, I'd like to hear from you and hope that you could take some time to post a review on Amazon. Your feedback and support will help this author to greatly improve his writing craft for future projects and make this book even better.

You can follow this link to *Little Poems* now.
I want you, the reader, to know that your review is very important and so, if you'd like to **leave a review**, all you have to do is click **here** and away you go. I wish you all the best in your future success!